Malshis

by Ruth Owen

PowerKiDS press™

New York

Published in 2015 by The Rosen Publishing Group, Inc.
29 East 21st Street, New York, NY 10010

First Edition

Produced for Rosen by Ruby Tuesday Books Ltd
Editor for Ruby Tuesday Books Ltd: Mark J. Sachner
US Editor: Joshua Shadowens
Designer: Emma Randall

Photo Credits:
Cover, 1, 3, 4–5, 6–7, 8–9, 10–11, 12–13, 14–15, 16–17, 20–21, 22–23, 24–25, 27
(bottom), 28–29, 30 © Shutterstock; 18, 27 (top) © Alamy; 19 © Superstock.

Library of Congress Cataloging-in-Publication Data

Owen, Ruth, 1967– author.
 Malshis / by Ruth Owen. — First edition.
    pages cm. — (Designer dogs)
 Includes index.
 ISBN 978-1-4777-7027-6 (library binding) — ISBN 978-1-4777-7028-3 (pbk.) —
 ISBN 978-1-4777-7029-0 (6-pack)
 1. Malshi—Juvenile literature. 2. Toy dogs—Juvenile literature. [1. Dogs.]
 I. Title.
 SF429.M24O94 2015
 636.76—dc23

                              2014001192

Manufactured in the United States of America

CPSIA Compliance Information: Batch #WS14PK8: For Further Information contact Rosen Publishing, New York, New York at 1-800-237-9932

Contents

woof

Meet a Malshi

What has long, silky hair, can be quiet and gentle, or lively and playful? The answer is a malshi.

Malshis are a **crossbreed** dog. This means they are a mixture of two different dog **breeds**. When a Maltese and a Shih Tzu have puppies together, they make malshis.

Malshis have sweet, loving personalities. They are great pets for families with young children. A smart, gentle malshi will also be a good choice as a first-time dog for a person who has never owned a dog before.

Adult Maltese   Adult Shih Tzu   Malshi puppy

This malshi is three years old.

Malshi dogs have not been around for very long. Dog **breeders** only began breeding them in the 1990s.

5

What Is a Designer Dog?

The American Kennel Club is a club for dog breeders. The club's official list of dog breeds includes over 175 different breeds. Many of these breeds have been around for hundreds of years.

Designer dogs are new types of dogs that have only been around for 20 to 30 years. Designer dogs get their nickname because dog breeders designed, or created, them from two older breeds. These new crossbreed dogs have names made up from the names of their parents' breeds.

The name "malshi" is made up from the names "Maltese" and "Shih Tzu."

Malshi puppies

Meet some designer dogs

A cockapoo is a cross between a cocker spaniel and a poodle.

A puggle is a cross between a pug and a beagle.

A labradoodle is a cross between a Labrador and a poodle.

The Maltese breed belongs to a dog group known as "toy dogs." Toy dogs are small dogs that are bred especially to be **companions** to people. Maltese are happy, friendly, intelligent little dogs that can live for over 12 years.

Maltese have long, straight, silky, white hair that must be **groomed** every day. These dogs also need about 30 minutes of exercise each day.

Adult Maltese size

Weight = 4 to 6 pounds
(1.8 to 2.7 kg)

Height to shoulder:
10 inches (25 cm)

A Maltese puppy

Maltese may look too perfect and glamorous for play, but these lively pups love to have fun and play games with their owners.

Meet the Parents: Ancient Maltese

No one knows for sure how the Maltese breed came to be. Old records show that Maltese lived in countries around the Mediterranean Sea. This included the island of Malta, from where the breed may have gotten its name. In fact, ancient records show that Maltese dogs were living in Malta during Roman times.

In Egypt, a statue of a Maltese dog from ancient Egyptian times was found by **archaeologists**. This ancient **evidence** shows that these little dogs have been around for at least 2,000 years!

An adult Maltese groomed for a dog show

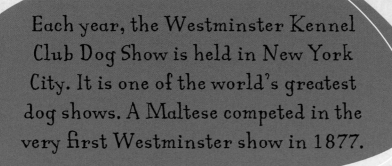

Each year, the Westminster Kennel Club Dog Show is held in New York City. It is one of the world's greatest dog shows. A Maltese competed in the very first Westminster show in 1877.

This Maltese is having her coat trimmed, or clipped, by a dog groomer.

Meet the Parents: Shih Tzu

Shih Tzus are a very popular breed in the United States. The American Kennel Club keeps a list of how many dogs are owned in each breed. In 2012, Shih Tzus were the eleventh most popular breed on the list. That was number 11 out of 175 different breeds!

Shih Tzus are loving, friendly dogs that are very trusting of people. They need to have up to one hour of exercise each day. Their long, thick coats must also be groomed every day. Shih Tzus can live for over 10 years.

Adult Shih Tzu size

Weight = 9 to 16 pounds (4 to 7 kg)

Height to shoulder: about 10 inches (25 cm)

A Shih Tzu's hair might be just one color, such as black or brown. It might also be white with markings that can be colors such as black, gold, red, gray, or brown.

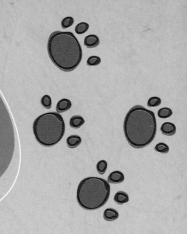

A gold and white Shih Tzu

A gray and white Shih Tzu

A black Shih Tzu

Meet the Parents: Lion Dogs

Shih Tzus have been around for many centuries. In China, these dogs were the favorites of Chinese royalty.

In the Buddhist faith of China, lions are very important creatures. Many Chinese buildings have statues of lions outside. These are guardian lions that are said to have mysterious, protective powers. Shih Tzus look a little like tiny lions. So the little "lion dogs" were thought to be living symbols of the guardian lions. Shih Tzus lived in palaces and temples and were the prized pets of Chinese emperors and empresses.

A little "lion dog"

A guardian lion statue outside the palaces of the Forbidden City in Beijing, China

In Chinese, the name "Shih Tzu" means "lion."

Malshi Looks

Just like its parents, a malshi will be a small dog. An adult malshi measures about 10 inches (25 cm) from the ground to its shoulders. When it is fully grown, a malshi should weigh no more than 10 pounds (4.5 kg).

A malshi has a long, silky coat. The hair is usually white with markings in black or brown.

The exciting thing about designer dogs is that it's hard to **predict** how they will look. A malshi might look more like one parent or be a mixture of both its parents!

A Shih Tzu

This malshi looks more like a Shih Tzu.

A Maltese

A malshi should live for 12 to 14 years.

A group of malshis

This malshi looks more like a Maltese.

Loving Malshis

Malshis are a mixture of their parents' personalities. This means they are happy, friendly, loving, trusting, and smart.

Malshis are happy to fit in with the lives of their human family. If a malshi lives with children, it will love to spend lots of time playing. If it lives with an elderly person, however, it will be happy to live a quieter life. As long as it gets some exercise each day, time spent cuddled up on its owner's lap will do just fine!

A malshi having fun with his owner

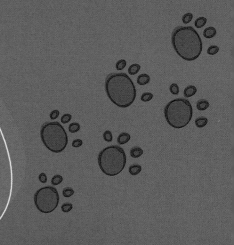

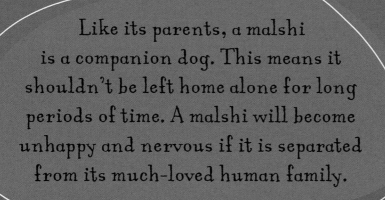

Like its parents, a malshi is a companion dog. This means it shouldn't be left home alone for long periods of time. A malshi will become unhappy and nervous if it is separated from its much-loved human family.

Malshi Pups

A malshi puppy may have a Maltese father and Shih Tzu mother, or the other way around.

The mother dog usually gives birth to about five puppies at one time. The tiny malshis are born with their eyes closed, and they cannot walk. The newborn pups spend all their time sleeping or drinking milk from their mother.

By the time it is four weeks old, however, each pup will be able to scamper around and play with its brothers and sisters.

When they are about five weeks old, the pups will start to eat solid food as well as drinking their mom's milk. They enjoy eating canned puppy food or cereal and milk.

A Shih Tzu mother dog

These malshi puppies are seven weeks old.

Buying a Puppy

If your family would like to own a malshi, you should only buy a puppy from a good dog breeder. So how can you be sure that a breeder is good and caring?

It's best to choose a puppy that has been raised in a breeder's home. A good breeder should be very happy for you to visit his or her house to see the puppies. The breeder should also be happy for you to meet the puppies' mother.

Puppies that are raised in a loving home will be used to being petted by people. They will not be afraid of humans.

Malshi puppies that are raised in a breeder's house won't be afraid of everyday noises such as vacuum cleaners and washing machines.

This happy pup has lots of toys to play with in its home.

Choosing a Puppy

It's exciting to visit a dog breeder's home to choose a puppy! Here are some tips on what to look for.

You might see a puppy that's very brave and is fighting with his brothers and sisters. You might also see a puppy that's very shy and hides from you. It's best to go for a puppy that is not too brave and not too shy. Choose a puppy that is playful, but gentle, and seems interested in meeting you.

Which malshi puppy would you choose?

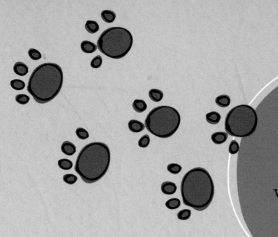

Once you have chosen a puppy, it will be able to come live with you when it is nine weeks old. Before that age, the little pup needs its mom.

Caring for a Malshi

A malshi should have at least 15 minutes of exercise each day. This could be a walk in the park or a game of fetch in a yard, or even along an apartment hallway.

Ask the breeder or your vet what foods are best to give your dog and how much to feed him or her. Divide your dog's food into two meals each day. Feed your dog at the same two times every day, too, as dogs like **routine**.

Caring owners make sure their dogs don't get overweight. Dogs can be greedy and will often ask for more food—even if they don't need it!

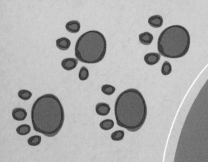

Here's how to make sure your dog isn't overweight.

• Look at your dog from above. You should be able to see a waist between its chest and hips.

• Place your hands on the sides of its chest. You should be able to feel its ribs.

If you think your dog might be overweight, visit your vet, who will be able to advise on a doggie diet.

A Malshi's Beauty Routine

A malshi's long, silky coat needs to be groomed every day. You can ask a dog groomer to clip your dog's coat so it's shorter. It will still need brushing once a week, though.

If you can hear your dog's toenails tapping on the floor, they're too long. Ask a dog groomer or your vet to trim the dog's nails.

Get your new puppy used to a grooming routine. Gently brush the puppy's hair. Touch the puppy's feet, too. Then, when it's time for a beauty treatment, your malshi won't be scared.

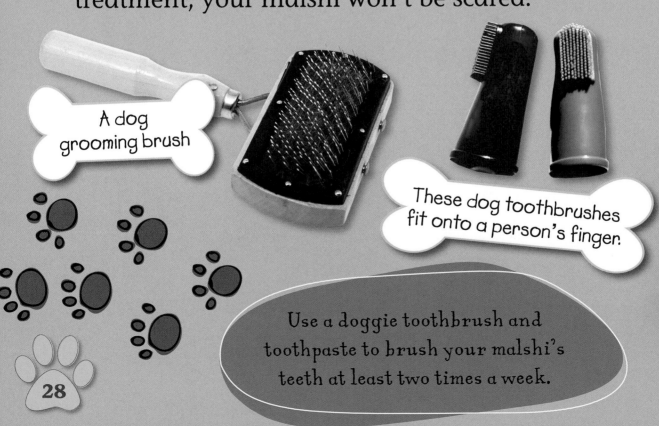

A dog grooming brush

These dog toothbrushes fit onto a person's finger.

Use a doggie toothbrush and toothpaste to brush your malshi's teeth at least two times a week.

A malshi puppy

Glossary

archaeologists (ahr-kee-AH-luh-jists) Scientists who study the past by examining the remains left behind of old buildings, skeletons, and objects such as statues.

breeders (BREE-derz) People who breed animals, such as dogs, and sell them.

breeds (BREEDZ) Different types of dogs. The word "breed" is also used to describe the act of mating two dogs in order for them to have puppies.

companions (kum-PAN-yunz) People or animals with whom one spends a lot of time.

crossbreed
(KROS-breed)
A type of dog created
from two different breeds.

evidence
(EH-vuh-dents)
Something that can prove
or disprove a fact.

groomed (GROOMD)
Cleaned by brushing
or washing.

predict (prih-DIKT)
To make a careful guess
about something.

routine (roo-TEEN) A
series of actions that
happen at the same time
each day.

Websites
Due to the changing nature
of Internet links, PowerKids Press has
developed an online list of websites related to the
subject of this book. This site is updated regularly.
Please use this link to access the list:

www.powerkidslinks.com/ddog/malshi/

Read More

Burstein, John. *Dogs*. Slim Goodbody's Inside Guide to Pets. New York: Gareth Stevens, 2008.

Larrew, Brekka Hervey. *Shih Tzus*. All About Dogs. Mankato, MN: Capstone Press, 2009.

Trueit, Trudi Strain. *Veterinarian*. Careers with Animals. New York: Cavendish Square Publishing, 2014.

Index